I0558141

BOOK CLUB

JOURNAL FOR READERS

This journal belongs to:

TITLE		DATE	PAGES
AUTHOR			

TITLE		DATE	PAGES
AUTHOR			

TITLE		DATE	PAGES
AUTHOR			

TITLE		DATE	PAGES
AUTHOR			

TITLE		DATE	PAGES
AUTHOR			

TITLE		DATE	PAGES
AUTHOR			

Notes:

TITLE	DATE	PAGES
AUTHOR		

TITLE	DATE	PAGES
AUTHOR		

TITLE	DATE	PAGES
AUTHOR		

TITLE	DATE	PAGES
AUTHOR		

TITLE	DATE	PAGES
AUTHOR		

TITLE	DATE	PAGES
AUTHOR		

Notes:

TITLE   DATE   PAGES

AUTHOR

TITLE   DATE   PAGES

AUTHOR

TITLE   DATE   PAGES

AUTHOR

TITLE   DATE   PAGES

AUTHOR

TITLE   DATE   PAGES

AUTHOR

TITLE   DATE   PAGES

AUTHOR

Notes:

TITLE		DATE	PAGES
AUTHOR			
TITLE		DATE	PAGES
AUTHOR			
TITLE		DATE	PAGES
AUTHOR			
TITLE		DATE	PAGES
AUTHOR			
TITLE		DATE	PAGES
AUTHOR			
TITLE		DATE	PAGES
AUTHOR			

Notes:

TITLE   DATE   PAGES

AUTHOR

TITLE   DATE   PAGES

AUTHOR

TITLE   DATE   PAGES

AUTHOR

TITLE   DATE   PAGES

AUTHOR

TITLE   DATE   PAGES

AUTHOR

TITLE   DATE   PAGES

AUTHOR

Notes:

Book Club Selection

Book title	*Author*	*Genre*

Plot

Setting/Time

Characters

Themes & Motifs

Discussion Questions or Topics:

Book Review & Reflection

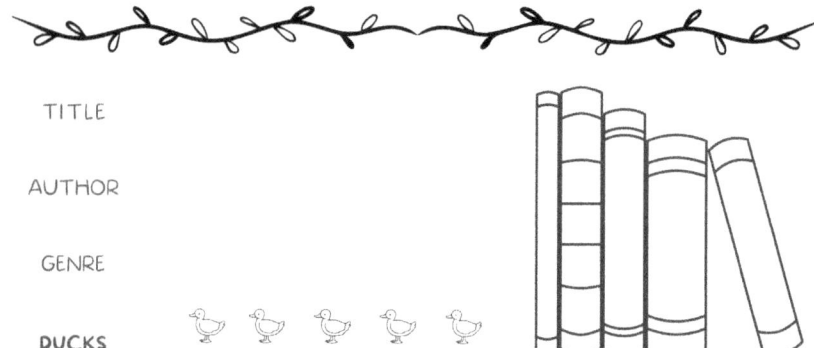

TITLE

AUTHOR

GENRE

DUCKS

QUESTIONS

FAVORITE MOMENT OR CHAPTER

Other Thoughts

ook Summary

TITLE	
AUTHOR	
SETTING	
PROTAGONIST	

SUMMARY

BY	
QUOTE	

BY	
QUOTE	

BY	
QUOTE	

BY	
QUOTE	

BY	
QUOTE	

to do List

- ☐ ....
- ☐ ....
- ☐ ....
- ☐ ....
- ☐ ....
- ☐ ....
- ☐ ....
- ☐ ....
- ☐ ....
- ☐ ....

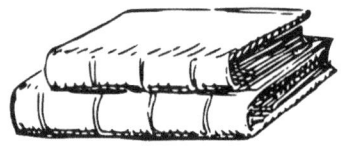

Book Club Selection

Book title	*Author*	*Genre*

Plot

Setting/Time

Characters

Themes & Motifs

Discussion Questions or Topics:

Book Review & Reflection

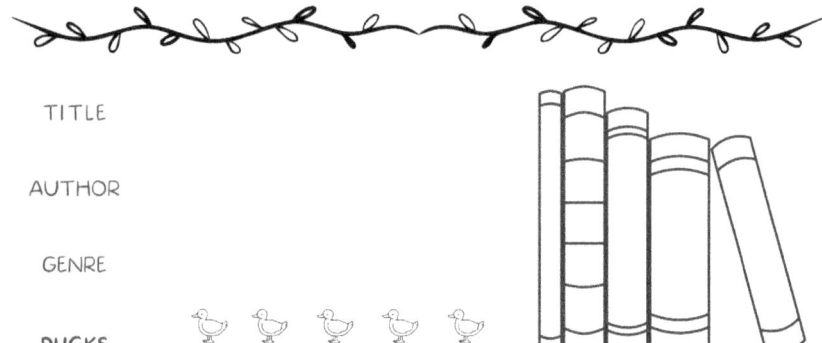

TITLE

AUTHOR

GENRE

DUCKS

QUESTIONS

FAVORITE MOMENT OR CHAPTER

Other Thoughts

ook Summary

TITLE	
AUTHOR	
SETTING	
PROTAGONIST	

SUMMARY

BY

QUOTE

BY

QUOTE

BY

QUOTE

BY

QUOTE

BY

QUOTE

_____

_____

_____

_____

_____

_____

_____

_____

_____

_____

_____

_____

_____

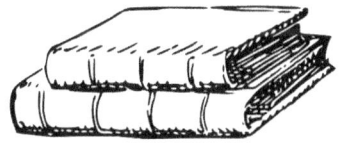

_____

_____

_____

_____

_____

_____

_____

_____

_____

_____

_____

_____

to do List

- ☐ ....
- ☐ ....
- ☐ ....
- ☐ ....
- ☐ ....
- ☐ ....
- ☐ ....
- ☐ ....
- ☐ ....
- ☐ ....

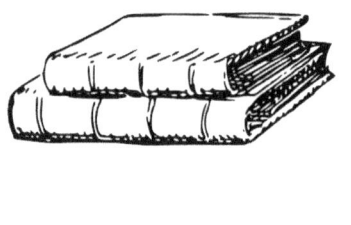

_____

_____

_____

_____

_____

_____

_____

_____

_____

_____

_____

_____

Book Club Selection

_____   _____   _____
Book title   *Author*   *Genre*

Plot   Setting/Time

....
....
....
....
....

Characters   Themes & Motifs

....
....
....
....

Discussion Questions or Topics:

Book Review & Reflection

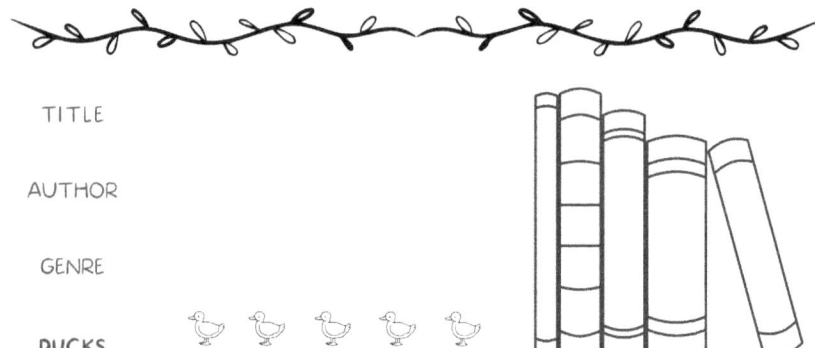

TITLE

AUTHOR

GENRE

DUCKS

QUESTIONS

FAVORITE MOMENT OR CHAPTER

Other Thoughts

ook Summary

TITLE	
AUTHOR	
SETTING	
PROTAGONIST	

SUMMARY

BY

QUOTE

BY

QUOTE

BY

QUOTE

BY

QUOTE

BY

QUOTE

_____
_____
_____
_____
_____
_____
_____
_____
_____
_____
_____
_____
_____

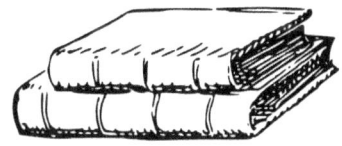

_____

_____

_____

_____

_____

_____

_____

_____

_____

_____

_____

_____

to do List

- ☐ ....
- ☐ ....
- ☐ ....
- ☐ ....
- ☐ ....
- ☐ ....
- ☐ ....
- ☐ ....
- ☐ ....
- ☐ ....

_____

_____

_____

_____

_____

_____

_____

_____

_____

_____

_____

_____

_____

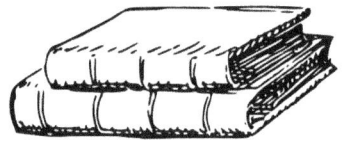

Book Club Selection

| Book title | Author | Genre |

Plot

Setting/Time

Characters

Themes & Motifs

Discussion Questions or Topics:

Book Review & Reflection

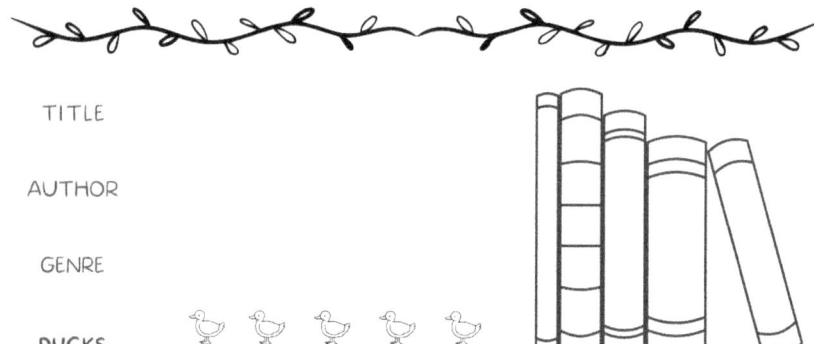

TITLE

AUTHOR

GENRE

DUCKS

QUESTIONS

FAVORITE MOMENT OR CHAPTER

Other Thoughts

ook Summary

TITLE	
AUTHOR	
SETTING	
PROTAGONIST	

SUMMARY

BY

QUOTE

BY

QUOTE

BY

QUOTE

BY

QUOTE

BY

QUOTE

_____

_____

_____

_____

_____

_____

_____

_____

_____

_____

_____

_____

_____

_____

_____

_____

_____

_____

_____

_____

_____

_____

_____

_____

_____

_____

_____

_____

_____

_____

_____

_____

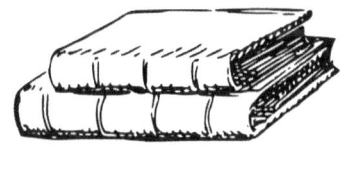

to do List

- ☐ ....
- ☐ ....
- ☐ ....
- ☐ ....
- ☐ ....
- ☐ ....
- ☐ ....
- ☐ ....
- ☐ ....
- ☐ ....

_____

_____

_____

_____

_____

_____

_____

_____

_____

_____

_____

_____

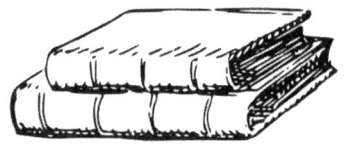

Book Club Selection

Book title   **Author**   **Genre**

Plot

Setting/Time

Characters

Themes & Motifs

Discussion Questions or Topics:

Book Review & Reflection

TITLE

AUTHOR

GENRE

DUCKS

QUESTIONS

FAVORITE MOMENT OR CHAPTER

Other Thoughts

TITLE	
AUTHOR	
SETTING	
PROTAGONIST	

SUMMARY

BY

QUOTE

BY

QUOTE

BY

QUOTE

BY

QUOTE

BY

QUOTE

_____

_____

_____

_____

_____

_____

_____

_____

_____

_____

_____

_____

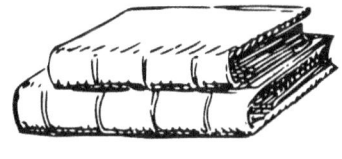

_____

_____

_____

_____

_____

_____

_____

_____

_____

_____

_____

_____

to do List

- ☐ ....
- ☐ ....
- ☐ ....
- ☐ ....
- ☐ ....
- ☐ ....
- ☐ ....
- ☐ ....
- ☐ ....
- ☐ ....

_____

_____

_____

_____

_____

_____

_____

_____

_____

_____

_____

_____

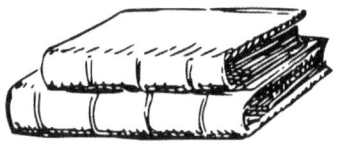

_____

_____

_____

_____

_____

_____

_____

_____

_____

_____

_____

_____

Book Club Selection

Book title   Author   Genre

Plot

Setting/Time

Characters

Themes & Motifs

Discussion Questions or Topics:

Book Review & Reflection

TITLE

AUTHOR

GENRE

DUCKS

QUESTIONS

FAVORITE MOMENT OR CHAPTER

Other Thoughts

ook Summary

TITLE	
AUTHOR	
SETTING	
PROTAGONIST	

SUMMARY

BY

QUOTE

BY

QUOTE

BY

QUOTE

BY

QUOTE

BY

QUOTE

_____

_____

_____

_____

_____

_____

_____

_____

_____

_____

_____

_____

to do List

- ☐ ....
- ☐ ....
- ☐ ....
- ☐ ....
- ☐ ....
- ☐ ....
- ☐ ....
- ☐ ....
- ☐ ....
- ☐ ....

_____

_____

_____

_____

_____

_____

_____

_____

_____

_____

_____

_____

_____

_____

_____

_____

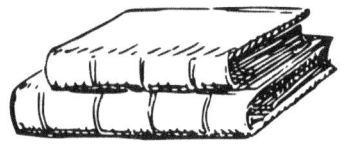

Book Club Selection

_____   _____   _____
Book title   *Author*   *Genre*

Plot

Setting/Time

Characters

Themes & Motifs

Discussion Questions or Topics:

Book Review & Reflection

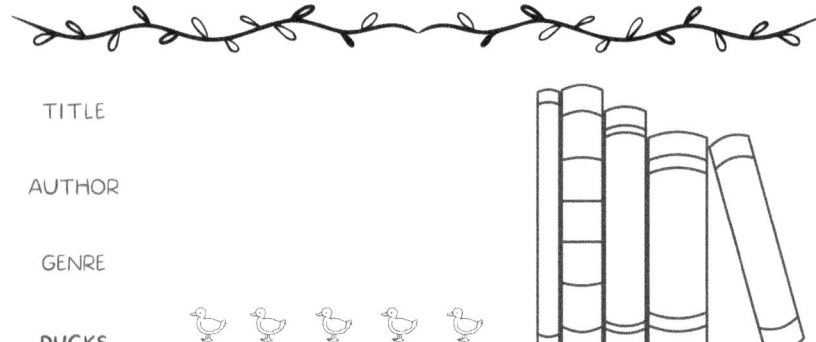

TITLE

AUTHOR

GENRE

DUCKS

QUESTIONS

FAVORITE MOMENT OR CHAPTER

Other Thoughts

ook Summary

TITLE	
AUTHOR	
SETTING	
PROTAGONIST	

SUMMARY

BY	
QUOTE	
BY	
QUOTE	
BY	
QUOTE	
BY	
QUOTE	
BY	
QUOTE	

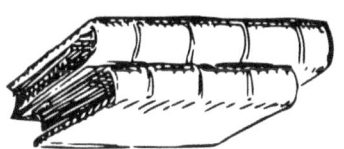

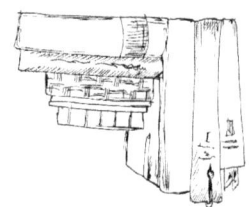

· ☐

· ☐

· ☐

· ☐

· ☐

· ☐

· ☐

· ☐

· ☐

· ☐

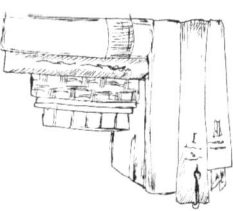

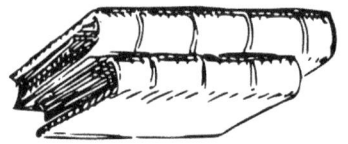

Book Club Selection

<u>Book title</u>

<u>Author</u>

<u>Genre</u>

Plot

Setting/Time

Characters

Themes & Motifs

Discussion Questions or Topics:

Book Review & Reflection

TITLE

AUTHOR

GENRE

DUCKS

QUESTIONS

FAVORITE MOMENT OR CHAPTER

Other Thoughts

ook Summary

TITLE	
AUTHOR	
SETTING	
PROTAGONIST	

SUMMARY

QUOTE

BY

QUOTE

BY

QUOTE

BY

QUOTE

BY

QUOTE

BY

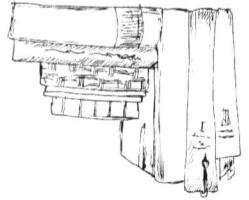

.... ☐

.... ☐

.... ☐

.... ☐

.... ☐

.... ☐

.... ☐

.... ☐

.... ☐

.... ☐

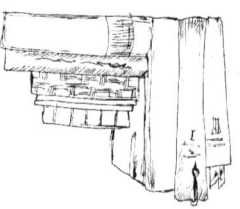

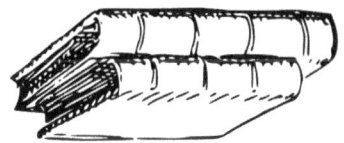

Book Club Selection

Book title	Author	Genre

Plot

Setting/Time

Characters

Themes & Motifs

Discussion Questions or Topics:

Book Review & Reflection

TITLE

AUTHOR

GENRE

DUCKS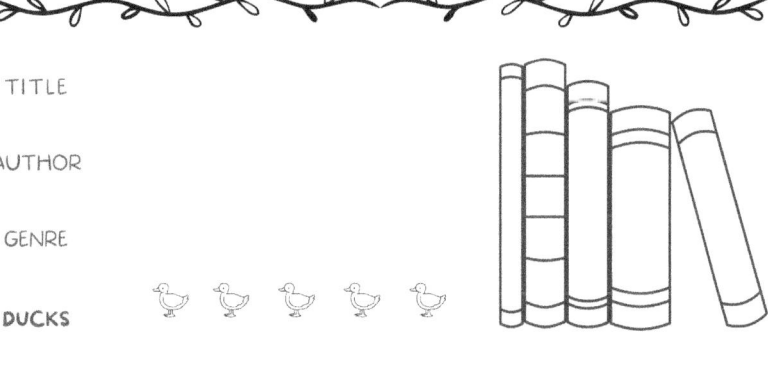

QUESTIONS

FAVORITE MOMENT OR CHAPTER

Other Thoughts

Book Summary

TITLE	
AUTHOR	
SETTING	
PROTAGONIST	

SUMMARY

QUOTE

BY

QUOTE

BY

QUOTE

BY

QUOTE

BY

QUOTE

BY

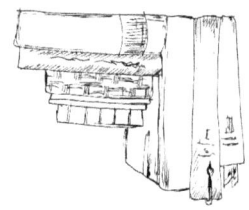

.... ☐

.... ☐

.... ☐

.... ☐

.... ☐

.... ☐

.... ☐

.... ☐

.... ☐

.... ☐

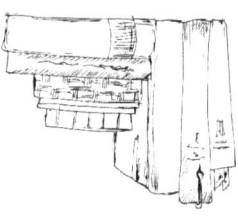

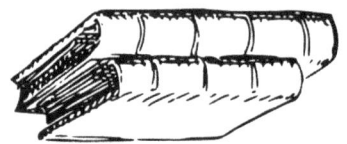

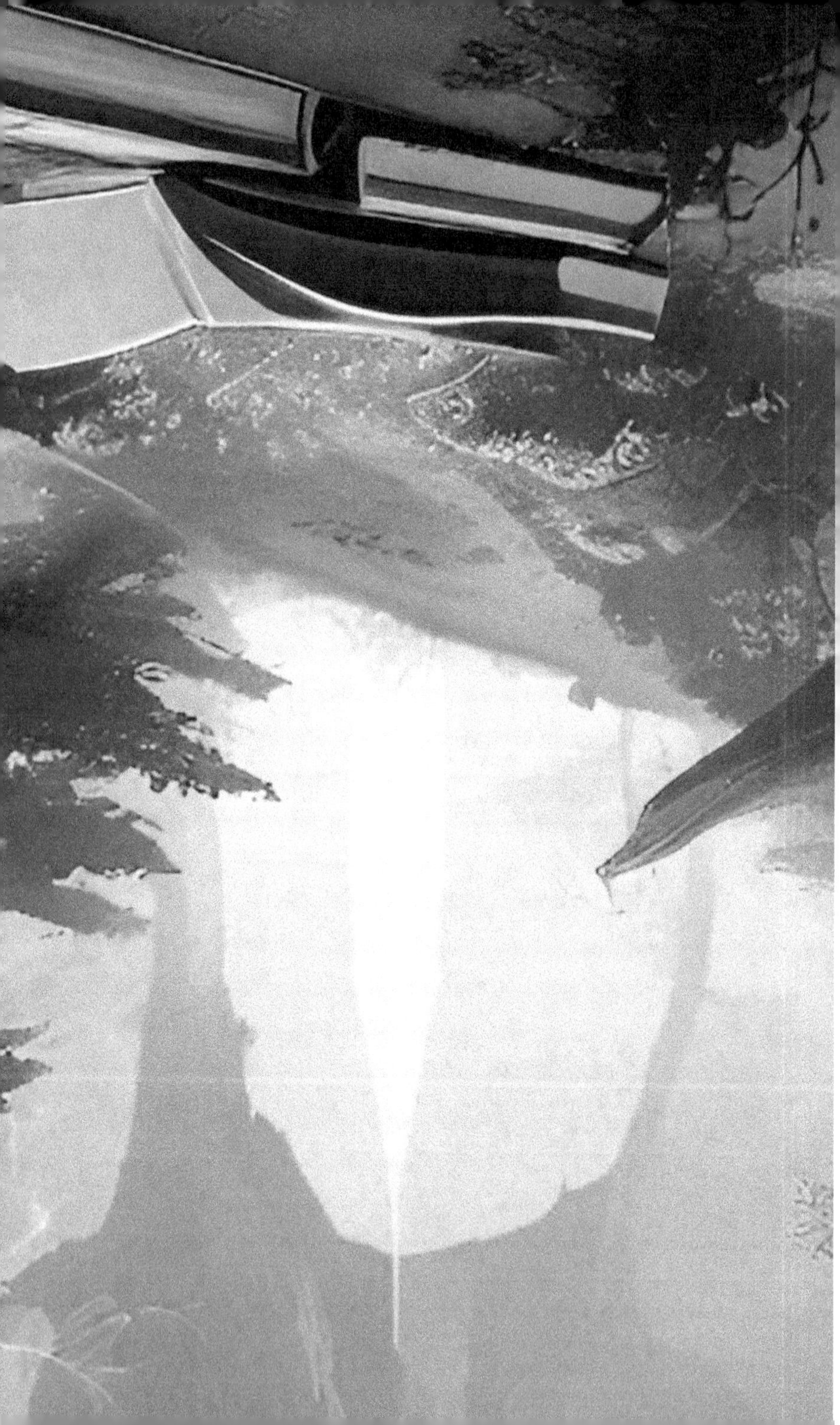

Book Club Selection

_____ _____ _____
Book title *Author* *Genre*

Plot

Setting/Time

Characters

Themes & Motifs

Discussion Questions or Topics:

Book Review & Reflection

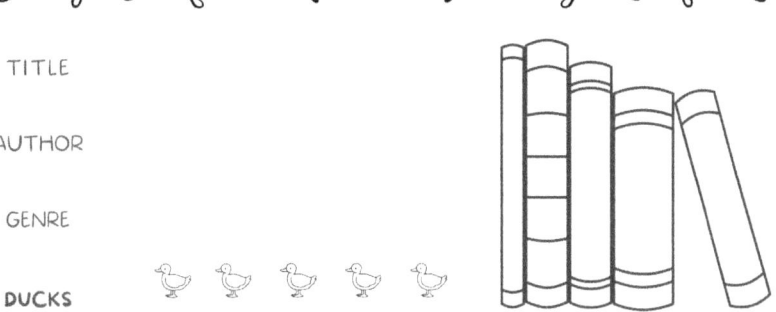

TITLE

AUTHOR

GENRE

DUCKS

QUESTIONS

FAVORITE MOMENT OR CHAPTER

Other Thoughts

TITLE	
AUTHOR	
SETTING	
PROTAGONIST	

SUMMARY

BY

QUOTE

BY

QUOTE

BY

QUOTE

BY

QUOTE

BY

QUOTE

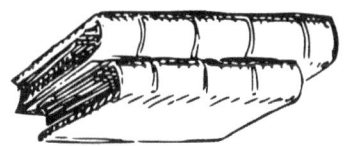

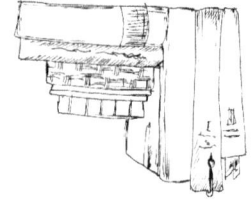

.... ☐

.... ☐

.... ☐

.... ☐

.... ☐

.... ☐

.... ☐

.... ☐

.... ☐

.... ☐

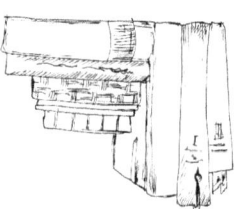

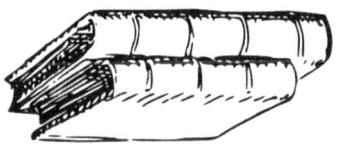

Book Club Contact

NAME	
PHONE	
EMAIL	
NAME	
PHONE	
EMAIL	
NAME	
PHONE	
EMAIL	
NAME	
PHONE	
EMAIL	
NAME	
PHONE	
EMAIL	

ook Club Contact

NAME	
PHONE	
EMAIL	
NAME	
PHONE	
EMAIL	
NAME	
PHONE	
EMAIL	
NAME	
PHONE	
EMAIL	
NAME	
PHONE	
EMAIL	

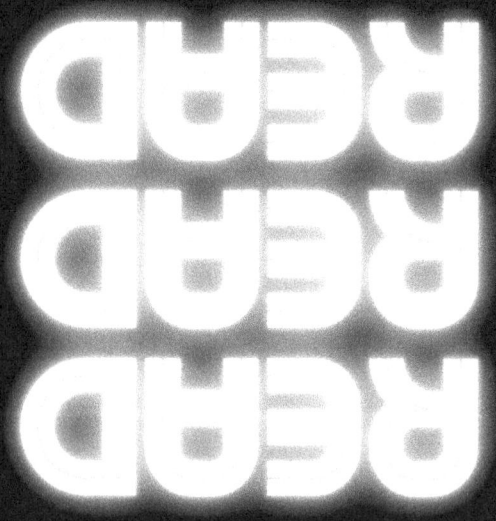

BOOK CLUB

JOURNAL FOR READERS

by Marya Patrice Sherron

www.ingramcontent.com/pod-product-compliance
Lightning Source LLC
Chambersburg PA
CBHW071005120626
46546CB00003B/936